Developing Literacy NON-FICTION

READING AND WRITING ACTIVITIES FOR THE LITERACY HOUR

year

Christine Moorcroft

Series consultant: Ray Barker

A & C BLACK

Contents

Writing composition

Published 2002 by
A & C Black (Publishers) Limited
37 Soho Square, London W1D 3QZ

ISBN 0-7136-6066-X

The author and publishers would like to thank Ray Barker, Madeleine Madden, Julia Tappin and Sarah Vickers for their advice in producing this series of books.

A CIP catalogue record for this book is available from the British Library.

Printed in Great Britain by The Cromwell Press Ltd, Trowbridge, Wiltshire

Introduction

Developing Literacy: Non-fiction is a series of seven photocopiable activity books for the Literacy Hour. Each book provides a range of non-fiction reading and writing activities, and supports the teaching of literacy skills at text, sentence and word levels.

The activities are designed to be carried out in the time allocated to independent work during the Literacy Hour. They incorporate strategies which encourage independent learning: for example, ways in which children can evaluate their own work or that of a partner.

The reading activities develop the children's study and research skills (reading for a purpose, understanding and interpreting, and making use of what they have read) and provide models on which they can base their own writing.

The writing activities concentrate on the purpose of a text, the audience for whom it is written and the context in which it is to be read, and encourage the children to be aware of these considerations when they write.

The activities in **Year 2** reinforce word-level and sentence-level skills and encourage the children to:

- read, follow, organise and write instructions;
- use and compile dictionaries, glossaries and other alphabetically organised texts;
- read and construct flow-charts and diagrams for explanation;
- distinguish between fact and fiction, and fiction and non-fiction;
- write questions and locate the answers in non-fiction texts by using the structural features of the texts (contents page, index, headings, sub-headings, captions and key words and phrases);
- skim-read, evaluate and make notes on non-fiction texts;
- using models from their reading, write non-fiction texts, including non-chronological reports.

The National Literacy Strategy and non-fiction

The National Literacy Strategy *Framework for Teaching* encourages teachers to use all kinds of non-fiction texts, both printed and electronic: for example, information texts; dictionaries; directories, catalogues and handbooks; CD-ROMs; leaflets; labels and captions in the classroom; and instructions which the children follow at school, at home and elsewhere.

Links to other subjects

The children can use their literacy skills to further their learning in other subjects, through the reading of shared texts or guided reading during the Literacy Hour and by using and developing their research skills at other times. During the Literacy Hour, the children can write about what they have learned in other subjects and learn how to select the best methods for their writing.

Using non-fiction in the Literacy Hour

While the activities in this book focus on the independent part of the Literacy Hour, the notes on pages 6 to 8 and at the foot of each activity page suggest a variety of ways you can introduce non-fiction reading and writing, present whole-class activities and use the plenary session to conclude the lesson. The ideas support the following strategies:

- **demonstrating** or modelling the way in which an experienced reader and writer tackles a skill or approach to reading or writing, by 'thinking aloud' about what you are doing;
- **sharing** an activity: the teacher or other adult (as the expert) takes responsibility for the difficult parts of the activity, while the learners take responsibility for the easier parts. The learners then gradually take over some of the more difficult parts. This bridges the gap between demonstration and independent work;
- **supporting** an activity, in which the children undertake the activity independently, with the teacher (or other adult) monitoring and being ready to offer support when necessary. This avoids the difficulties which arise when the teacher moves from demonstration or modelling to asking the children to work independently.

Children will benefit from learning the following strategies to help them read and write non-fiction:

- **predicting** (suggesting what information a book or page might provide, and how they can tell);
- **clarifying** (working out ways to understand new or difficult words and ideas);
- **questioning** (saying what questions the text raises; what it makes them want to find out);
- **summarising** (saying in a limited number of words what the text is about and what it tells them).

The activities in this book support the following stages of the children's interactions with text:

- **bringing to mind what they already know** about the subject (for example, making flow-charts, diagrams and lists);
- **deciding what they want to find out** (for example, writing questions);
- **deciding where to find the information they need** (for example, information books, electronic texts, people and websites);
- **learning the best ways in which to use the source** (from the teacher or other adult, who models the use of the source);
- **developing strategies to help them understand the text** (for example, marking difficult words or passages, re-phrasing, or transferring information from prose to charts or from diagrams to prose);
- **recording information** (using charts and note-making strategies such as abbreviation);
- **evaluating the information** (for example, evaluating the validity of the source or comparing information from different sources, and separating facts from opinions);
- **communicating information** (considering the audience, purpose and context of the text to be written and their effects on language and layout).

Reading

Most children will be able to carry out the activities independently. Children are not expected to be able to read all the instructions; it is assumed that the teacher or another adult will read to or with the children. As children gradually become accustomed to seeing instructions, they learn their purpose long before they can read them.

Extension activities

Most of the activity sheets end with a challenge (**Now try this!**) which reinforces and extends the children's learning and provides the teacher with an opportunity for assessment. These more challenging activities might be appropriate for only a few children; it is not expected that the whole class should complete them.

On some pages there is space for the children to complete the extension activities, but for others they will need a notebook or a separate sheet of paper.

Organisation

The activities require very few resources besides scissors, glue, word-banks and simple dictionaries. Other materials are specified in the teachers' notes on the activity pages.

Notes on the activities

The notes below expand upon those which are provided at the foot of each activity page. They give ideas and suggestions for making the most of the activity sheet, including suggestions for the whole-class introduction, the plenary session or for follow-up work using an adapted version of the activity sheet. To help teachers select appropriate learning experiences for their pupils, the activities are grouped into sections within the book, but the pages need not be presented in the order in which they appear, unless otherwise stated.

Reading comprehension

The activities in this section reinforce the children's word-level and sentence-level skills and develop their ability to read, use and understand the structure and language style of instructions, as well as use dictionaries, glossaries, indexes and other alphabetical texts. The activities encourage the children to plan their work by formulating questions and locating the answers efficiently in non-fiction texts. They help the children to distinguish between fact and fiction, and fiction and non-fiction. The children learn how to decide whether or not a non-fiction book will provide the information they want, then to scan the book to find that information and to skim-read before deciding which parts to read in detail.

Car park machine (page 9). This activity reinforces the children's skills in reading instructions. Encourage them to use the pictures as cues to help them read any words they do not know and to use the critical features of the words, such as familiar letter combinations (for example 'ou' and 'ch'). Read out the following sentences and ask the children whether they are instructions: 'I put my ticket in the machine,' 'I read how much to pay,' and 'I put my money in the slot.' Ask them to explain how they can tell. The activities on pages 29–32 allow the children to write instructions for other people to follow.

Bring and buy sale (page 10). This activity develops the children's understanding of how plans can be useful. Discuss what might happen at the bring and buy sale if there were no plan (you could ask them how the children holding the sale would know what to ask people to bring to the sale, where each stall should be, what would be sold at each stall and who should look after it).

Make a chain of people and **Learn to cut wood** (pages 11 and 12). These activities help children to recognise the critical features of instructions: a statement of purpose at the beginning, followed by a list of things needed, and then a step-by-step list of things to do (which uses direct language), along with diagrams to help explain them. The activity on page 33 encourages the children to organise the instructions they write and to use diagrams.

Use a dictionary (page 13). This activity shows the children how to use a dictionary efficiently to check spellings. Point out useful features in a dictionary such as alphabetical markers on the top, bottom or outside edge of the pages, and the guide words in bold (or in colour) at the tops of the pages. On an alphabet strip displayed in the classroom, the children could indicate where the words belong. They could write words they come across in their reading on strips of paper and fix them on to the correct sections of the alphabet line. Encourage the children to use a dictionary routinely to check words they are not sure how to spell.

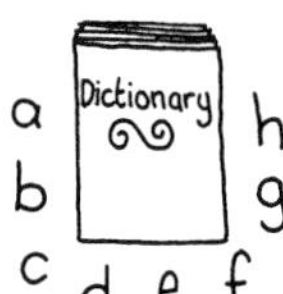

Look it up (page 14). This activity focuses on using a dictionary to find the meanings of words. In order to answer the questions, the children have to think about what they read in the dictionary definitions (which is not necessarily required when they merely look up and write out the meanings of words).

Definitions: 1 and 2 (pages 15–16). These pages reinforce the children's understanding of definitions and give practice in using a dictionary. The children may know some of the words in **Definitions: 1** but should use a dictionary to check that their understanding is correct. See also pages 35–36, which provide an opportunity to make a dictionary.

Use the index (page 17). This activity develops the children's skills in using an index for a purpose. They use the index of an information book to locate the pages on which they are likely to find the answers to questions. Useful information books for this activity include *Eyewitness Explorers: Weather* by John Farndon, Dorling Kindersley and *Usborne Spotters' Guides: The Weather* by Frances Wilson and Felicity Mansfield, Usborne. When introducing the activity, it is useful to help the children identify the key word in each question: for example, 'fog', 'clouds' and 'lightning'. Lower-achieving children may wish to copy the key word on to a strip of paper and move it down the index until they find the word that matches it.

Use the glossary (page 18). This activity encourages the children to use information books effectively, by looking up technical vocabulary connected with a topic. You could ask them questions about the information in the glossary: for example, 'What is the difference between a pond and a lake?', 'How is a river different from a canal?' and 'How is a mountain different from a hill?' Page 38 allows the children to make a glossary of their own.

Bo Peep's address book (page 19). This activity is based on a familiar alphabetically ordered text – an address book. You could introduce it by reading an enlarged copy of a real address book as a shared text. The entries are ordered by first letter only, since the user adds them to the next available space on the appropriate page. Let the children look at a collection of address books and talk about the features which make them easy to use, such as letter tabs at the edges of the pages or indented pages on which the initial letter can be seen without opening the book. The children could make their own address books and write in the addresses of their friends and family. You could introduce alphabetical order by both first and second letter by investigating what happens in a dictionary or other alphabetical list where two words begin with the same letter.

At the circus (page 20). This activity introduces the use of a flow-chart and diagrams in an explanation. It could be followed by **A giant's flow-chart** (page 39). Before they begin the activity, the children could read flow-charts in information books and then explain, in their own words, the process described in them.

A tomato plant (page 21). In this activity the children learn when it is appropriate to use a cyclical diagram in an explanation. They could first read other cyclical charts in science information books: for example, life-cycles of animals or plants and the water cycle. Discuss the important features of a cyclical diagram (labelled illustrations, boxes and arrows) and point out that it has no beginning or end. Ask the children if they can explain why not.

Fact or fiction? (page 22). This activity helps the children to distinguish between fact and fiction. They could write definitions of 'fact' and 'fiction' for display in the class library, with hints to help others decide whether a piece of text is fact or fiction. Useful words and phrases for this exercise include: 'real', 'made up', 'invented', 'true' and 'can be proved'.

Fiction or non-fiction? (page 23). This activity reinforces the differences between fiction and non-fiction books. Revise the terms 'fiction' and 'non-fiction' and invite children to choose a fiction book or a non-fiction book from a collection. Ask them how they can tell what kind of book it is, and point out the distinctive features of non-fiction books: the kind of title and front cover illustration, the back cover blurb, the contents page, the glossary and index and the layout of pages (including features such as labelled diagrams and charts).

What do you know? and **Finding out** (pages 24 and 25). These activities help the children to prepare for reading non-fiction for a purpose which is clear to them. They encourage the children to use information books to find specific pieces of information, having talked about what they already know about a topic. These activities can also allow the teacher to assess the children's understanding of a new topic in another subject (for example, science or geography) prior to beginning work on it. **Finding out** develops the children's skills in formulating questions before they read information texts. This process encourages them to use the texts to find specific information, and not to read them from beginning to end. The teacher can model how to evaluate information books as to their usefulness for answering a specific question by demonstrating how to check the contents page and index and then how to use them to locate the information. The children could go on to write the answers to their questions but the emphasis here is on preparation for reading.

What's the answer? (page 26). This activity shows the children how to use non-fiction books efficiently. Having decided what they want to find out, they learn to appraise books quickly, checking whether they are going to be helpful before they begin to read them. They could keep a checklist to hand when looking for information in any subject, reminding them to look at the title, contents page, headings, sub-headings, illustrations and index.

Find the information (page 27). This activity offers a useful strategy for reading for information. Rather than reading an information book from cover to cover, the children learn the steps to take to find the relevant parts of the book.

Text scan (page 28). This helps children develop the ability to scan a piece of text in order to find the relevant information efficiently.

Writing composition

These activities encourage the children to explore writing for different purposes: for example, instructions for getting from place to place, instructions for playing games and carrying out everyday activities, and recipes for making things. The children are encouraged to model their own writing on non-fiction texts they read. They learn to plan their writing of instructions, alphabetically ordered texts and non-chronological reports with the help of frameworks and models. They also learn to plan the structure and contents of their own books.

A journey (page 29). In this activity the children work out how someone can travel from one town to another using a combination of walking and travelling by bus and train. Before the activity you could take the children for a walk in the local area. As you walk, talk about the direction you are taking and the things you pass. Afterwards, describe the walk together: for example, 'We turned right at the school gate and walked along...'. Ask them to change what they say into instructions (to tell someone else what to do). The children could also write, and check for accuracy, instructions for visitors to the school.

Grotty soup (page 30). This activity presents a comic picture from which the children are required to gather information to write a recipe. They could check each other's recipes for omissions and for any parts which are in the wrong order.

Snakes and ladders and **Sending a letter** (pages 31 and 32). These activities provide the children with structures to help them write instructions for familiar processes, in the correct order and including all the important details.

Follow a diagram (page 33). This activity helps the children to use labelled drawings to convey information. For lower-achieving children, you could cut out the diagram for the children to glue on to a large piece of paper, allowing space for them to write their instructions next to the appropriate parts of it. Before the children begin the activity, they should look at labelled diagrams and pictures in books and notice how the diagrams are labelled: the labels are sometimes written in boxes and they are usually linked by lines to the parts they name. The children's instructions could be displayed for others to follow, then evaluate and suggest improvements.

Instruction words (page 34). This activity focuses on the language of instructions. The children examine the changes they need to make in order to turn a statement into an instruction. Similarly, they could convert into instructions any recounts they have previously written of things made during design and technology or art lessons.

Joke dictionary: 1 and 2 (pages 35–36). These pages develop the children's understanding of definitions and of how dictionaries are organised. The class could make a 'joke dictionary' of silly definitions using a scrap book in which the pages are lettered from A to Z.

Famous names (page 37). This activity allows the children to organise information from their work in history. All the historical figures depicted are from the National Curriculum exemplar scheme of work for history in Year 2.

Fairground glossary (page 38). This activity reinforces the children's skills in making lists and finding information from non-fiction texts, while developing their vocabulary. They could make glossaries for other collections, such as hats, shoes, reptiles, insects, countries and cities. This could be linked with sentence-level work on nouns.

A giant's flow-chart (page 39). This activity provides a framework to help the children write an explanation. The questions encourage them to organise their explanation and could be used as the basis for headings.

Gran's schooldays: 1 and 2 (pages 40–41). This activity shows how notes can be written quickly to help children remember information gathered. It also demonstrates how questions can be turned into sub-headings to support the organisation of a non-chronological report. Ask the children to choose questions they have written in preparation for reading about particular topics, then to turn the questions into sub-headings.

Making notes: 1 and 2 (pages 42–43). These pages develop skills in making notes as quickly and accurately as possible (using standard abbreviations). Children also practise identifying the parts of a text which are relevant to their questions. The activities discourage children from copying out of large pieces of text and help them to write 'in their own words'.

Topic word lists and **Silly lists** (pages 44 and 45). These activities present two different ways of writing lists: in a vertical, alphabetical format, without punctuation (as used in many topic word-banks) and in a horizontal format with the items separated by commas (except for the last two, which are separated by 'and').

Write a report (page 46). This activity involves planning and writing a non-chronological report. The children could first read a non-chronological report about a place, but with some of the words masked. Ask them to supply the missing words.

Using a chart (page 47). This activity provides a structure which enables the children to organise the information they find in books. Other possible buildings include house, palace, castle, library, shop, shed, office, warehouse, cinema and bungalow. The children could draw similar charts for collecting information on other topics. Discuss the ways in which the chart can be adapted for the extension activity: for instance, the children could collect the names of pieces of furniture used for different purposes: storage, seating, sleeping and to support things (for example, a table or a plant stand).

An experiment (page 48). This activity provides support for the writing of a simple chronological recount. It encourages the children to plan their writing and to relate events in the order in which they happened, using words related to time.

Car park machine

- **Read the** instructions.

1. Put your ticket in the slot.

2. Read how much to pay.

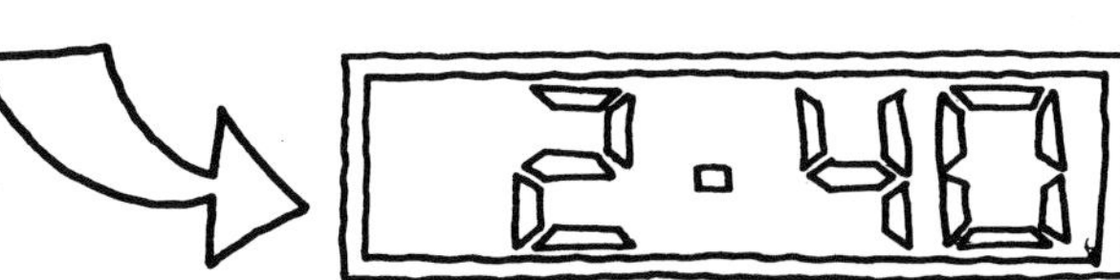

3. Put your money in the slot.

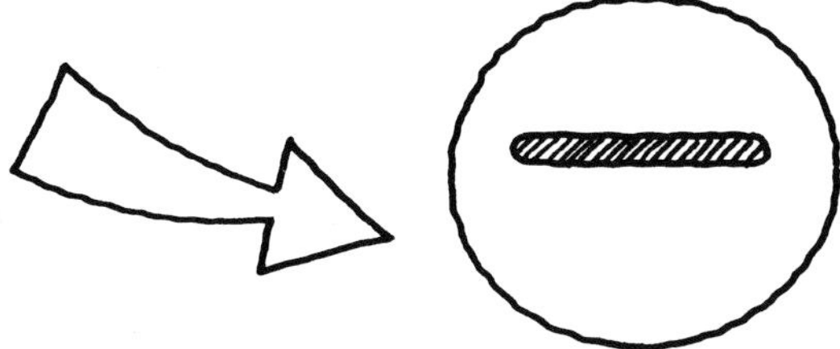

You can use these coins: £1, 50p, 20p, 10p, 5p.

No change given.

- **Answer the questions. Write** yes **or** no.

1. Do you need a ticket?
2. Is there a slot to put the ticket in?
3. Do you put the money in the same slot as the ticket?
4. Can you pay with 2p coins?

5. Can you pay with a £5 note?
6. Does change come out of a slot?

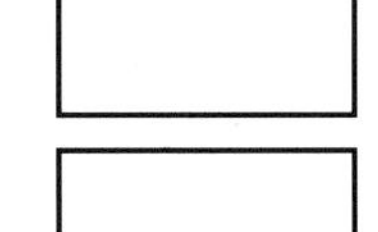

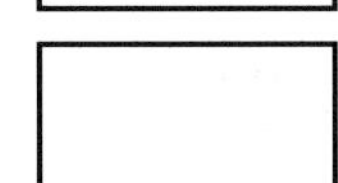

What else might you need to know about the car park?

- **Write three questions. Use** how, what **and** where.

This time, the answers will not be **yes** or **no**.

Teachers' note Ask the children if they have seen car park machines into which people insert money to pay for parking. Talk about how different machines work. Draw attention to the language of command used in instructions ('Put...', 'Read...' and so on).

Bring and buy sale

- **Look at the children's** plan.

- **Which child sells each item?**

a tin of soup	Adam
a cherry cake	__________
a jigsaw puzzle	__________
a jumper	__________
a cactus plant	__________
a ticket for the sale	__________
a dictionary	__________

- **Write three more questions about the bring and buy sale.**
- **Give them to a friend to answer.**

Teachers' note Discuss the children's experiences of bring and buy sales; ask what people buy there and where the things on sale come from. You could encourage the children to consider what they would bring in to sell if the class were to hold a bring and buy sale. Invite them to think about how they would organise their sale. Discuss and write the labels and signs which would be useful.

Make a chain of people

• **Follow the instructions.**

How to make a chain of people

You need:

a pencil

a strip of paper

scissors

1.

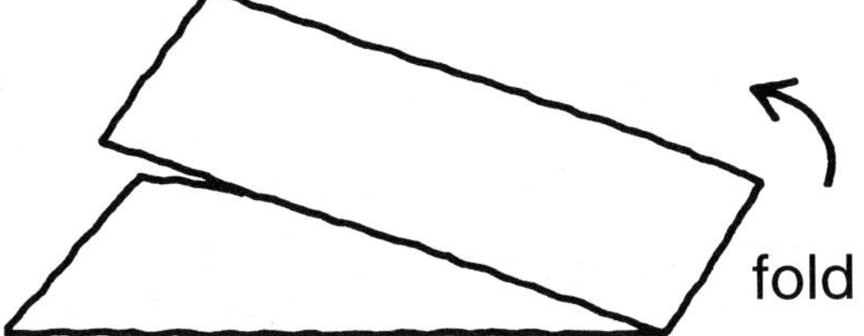

Fold the paper in half.

2.

Fold the paper in half again.

3.

Fold the paper in half again.

4.

Draw half a person on the fold.

5.

Do not cut along the folds!

Cut along the lines.

6.

Open out the chain of people.

• **Write about how easy or difficult it was to follow the instructions.**

Teachers' note You could introduce this activity by writing some simple instructions on the board: for example, for making sounds using a comb and tissue paper. The children could take turns to read out parts of the instructions for you to follow. Ask them to check that you do as they say (you could make some deliberate mistakes).

Learn to cut wood

- **Cut out the instructions.**
- **Put them in order.**

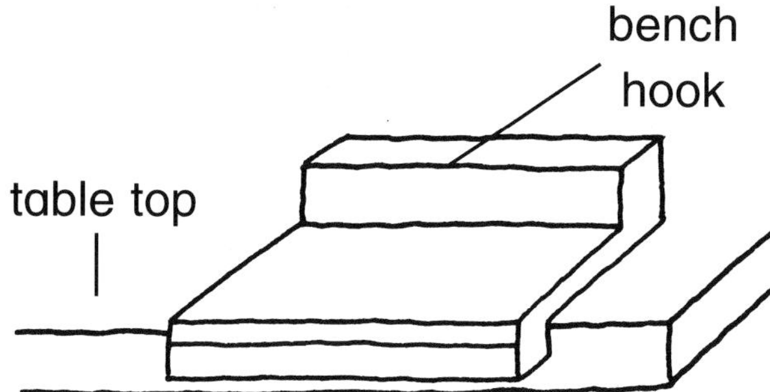

Put the bench hook on the table top.

Measure the wood.

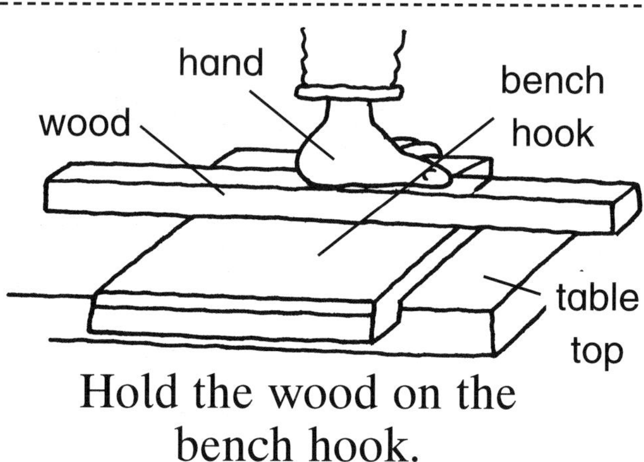

Hold the wood on the bench hook.

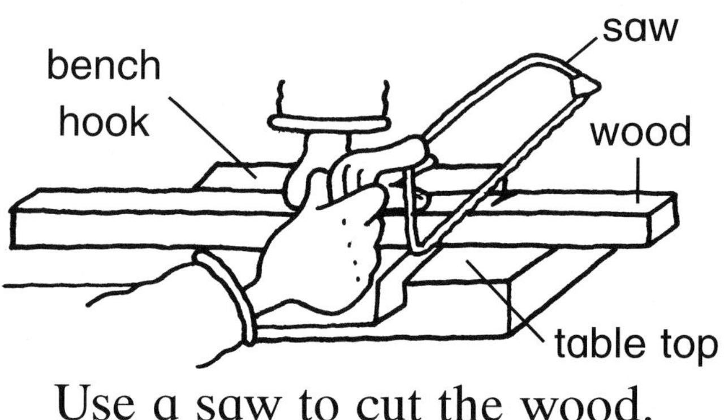

Use a saw to cut the wood.

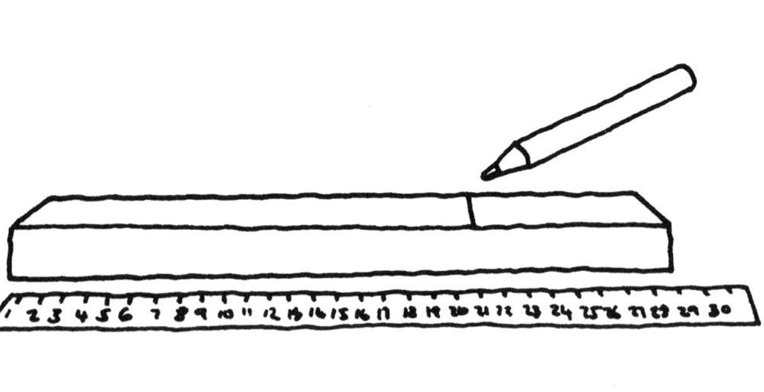

Mark the wood.

How to cut a piece of wood

You need:

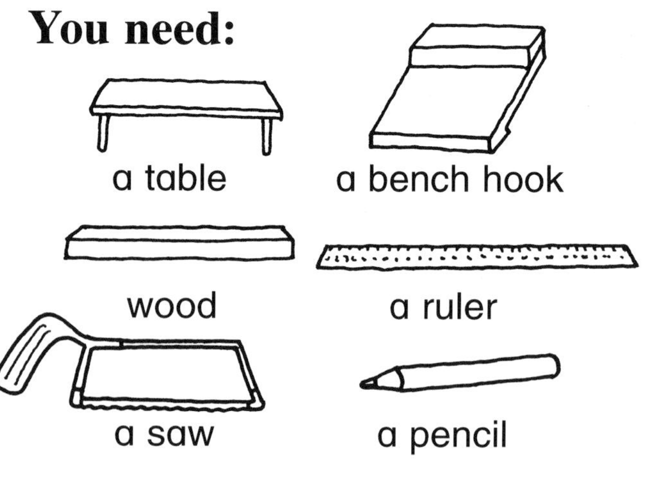

- **Write a safety warning for the instructions.**

Teachers' note Show the children the equipment depicted on the page and talk about how it is used (this might serve as an introduction to, or revision on, using these tools in design and technology lessons). Label and display the tools, so that the children can refer to them as they re-order the instructions.

Use a dictionary

a b c d e f g h	i j k l m n o p q r	s t u v w x y z
Near the front	**Near the middle**	**Near the back**

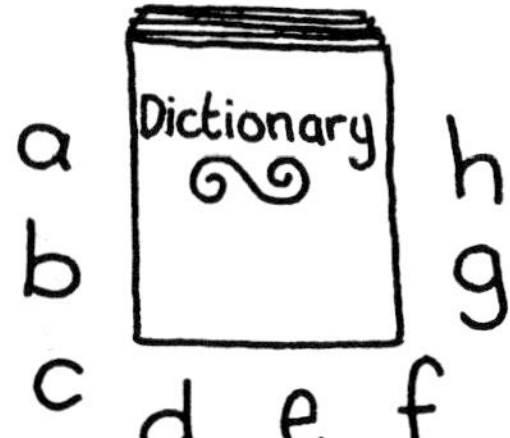

- **Look up the words.**
- **Complete the chart.**

- **Write the correct spellings in the last column.**

Word	Where will you look? front / middle / back	Is the spelling correct? ✓ ✗	Correct spelling
bear	front		
camel			
zebera			
monky			
sheap			
rabit			
aligator			
lion			

- **Write four words which you are not sure how to spell.**

__________ __________ __________ __________

- **Look them up in a dictionary.**
- **Write the correct spellings.**

__________ __________ __________ __________

Teachers' note Show the children a simple dictionary and ask them where you should open it to find, say, 'zip' (near the front/back/middle). Ask them how they know. Do the same with other examples and model how to find each word (by its first letter) within the chosen section. For the extension activity, emphasise that it does not matter if the children spell the words incorrectly the first time they write them.

Look it up

- **Look at the chart.**
- **Write the first letter of the word.**
- **Find the word in a dictionary.**
- **Answer the question.**

Word	First letter	Question	Yes or no
gorilla	g	Is this an animal?	
picture		Do people eat this?	
rugby		Is this a tree?	
add		Is this a colour?	
sandwich		Can you eat this?	
garage		Is a horse kept in it?	
mountain		Can you do this?	
dragon		Is this a monster?	
uniform		Do people wear this?	

Now try this!

- **Choose three words from the chart.**
- **Write their** definitions.

1. ______________________________

____

2. ______________________________

____

3. ______________________________

____

Teachers' note The children should first complete the activity on page 13. Revise how to find words alphabetically in the most appropriate section of the dictionary. For lower-achieving children you could cut out the words and show them how to move a word down the pages for that letter until they find the word that matches it.

Definitions 1

• **Match the words to their definitions.**

Use a dictionary.

Words

 jelly	owl	ice
 clown	 astronaut	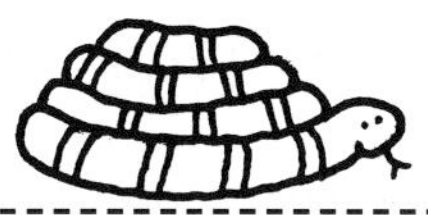 python
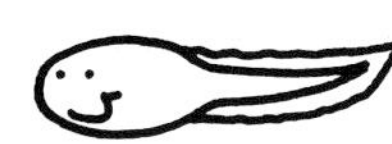 tadpole	 elf	 monster

Definitions

A large frightening creature found in stories.	Frozen water.	A person who travels in space.
A young frog or toad.	A circus actor who makes people laugh.	A sweet, wobbly food.
A tiny person in fairy tales.	A bird with a flat face and large eyes. It hunts small animals at night.	A kind of snake.

• **Put the words in alphabetical order, with their definitions.**

Teachers' note The children should first complete the activities on pages 13 and 14. As an introduction, give the children some words to find in a dictionary and ask them to read out their definitions. For the extension activity, you could give the children paper for them to glue the words and definitions on to: split the paper into 26 boxes and write each letter of the alphabet in a separate box.

Definitions 2

- **Read the definitions.**
- **Match them to the words.**
- **Write the words on the crossword.**

Use a dictionary.

Words

all
bird
birthday
draw
ear
kettle
key
rat
rice
rocket
tar
year
yellow

Across

1. The day you were born (8).
5. A food grain grown in hot, wet places (4).
6. Everything (3).
7. A pot with a lid and a spout, used for boiling water (6).
10. Twelve months (4).
11. A small mammal with sharp teeth and a long tail (3).

Down

1. An animal with a beak, feathers and wings (4).
2. A spacecraft with an engine (6).
3. To make a picture using a pencil (4).
4. The colour of a lemon (6).
7. A tool for opening locks (3).
8. Black sticky material used on roads (3).
9. Part of the body used for listening (3).

- **Write three words. Write their definitions.**
- **Mix them up. Ask a friend to match them.**

Teachers' note The children should first have completed the activities on pages 13–15. If necessary, explain how the answers on a crossword puzzle are numbered and point out why there is, say, no '2 across'. Model how to find and fill in the first answer.

Use the index

You need an information book about weather.

- **List the pages which will help you to answer the questions.**

Question	Pages
Where does fog come from?	
How are clouds made?	
What makes some clouds black?	
What happens when lightning strikes a building?	
What makes it rain?	
What makes the noise of thunder?	
What makes the wind blow?	
What is the shape of a snowflake?	

- **Write two more questions about weather.**

1. ______________________________

2. ______________________________

- **On which pages can you find the answers?**

Question 1 ______________ Question 2 ______________

- **Write the answers to your two questions.**

Teachers' note Show the children the index page of an information book and discuss its purpose. Model how to use the index to find information in answer to a question. Explain how the index is organised to make words easy to find and to show the pages on which they are mentioned. The same information book can be used for the extension as for the main activity.

Use the glossary

- **Find these words in the glossary.**
- **Underline them.**
- **Write the glossary word.**

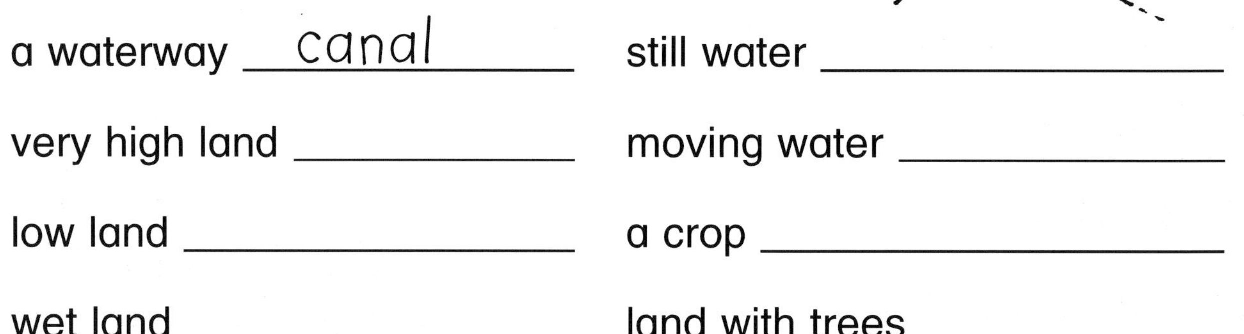

a waterway canal
very high land ______
low land ______
wet land ______
still water ______
moving water ______
a crop ______
land with trees ______

Glossary

canal A waterway which has been built as a route for transport.
forest A large area of land with trees.
hill A high piece of land (not as high as a mountain).
lake A large area of still water.
marsh A piece of very wet land.
motorway A road for traffic only.
mountain A very high piece of land.
oats A cereal crop, grown in fields for food.
pond A small area of still, fresh water.
river A large stream of moving water which flows through a valley until it joins another river, a lake or the sea.
valley A long piece of low land between hills or mountains.

- **Work with a friend.**

You each need a book with a glossary.

- **Write four words from your glossary.**
- **Ask your friend to find their meanings in the glossary.**

Teachers' note Provide information books with glossaries and model how to use the glossary to find the meaning of a word. It is useful to point out that a glossary, like a dictionary, gives definitions of words which are arranged in alphabetical order, but that it is easier to use than a dictionary because it gives only words included in that book.

Bo Peep's address book

Little Bo Peep keeps losing her friends' addresses!

- **Cut out the names and addresses.**
- **Put them in alphabetical order of family name.**
- **Glue them into an address book.**

Jack Horner
2 Plum Lane
Puddingtown

Bobby Shaftoe
The Sea House
Saltsea

Mother Hubbard
The Dog House
Boneville

Miss Muffet
The Tuffet
Spiderly

Humpty Dumpty
The Wall
Eggtown

Incey Wincey
The Spout
Spiderly

Dr Foster
1 Puddle Road
Not Gloucester

Peter Piper
3 Pickle Avenue
Pepperton

Lucy Locket
2 Lost Pocket Street
Ribbon

Jack Sprat
3 Fatfree Drive
Leantown

Teachers' note Help the children to make a simple address book, for example by folding in half two sheets of A4 paper and putting one inside the other (you could staple or glue the fold). Introduce the activity by writing on strips of paper the personal names of five children. With the class, put them in alphabetical order. Then add the family names, and discuss how to put them in order of family name.

At the circus

• **Read the circus act** flow-chart.

• **Write about the circus act. Fill in the gaps.**

1. Joey climbs ________ up some ________ and ________ on a platform. Coco stands on one end of a ________.

2. Joey ________ down on to the other ______ of the see-saw.

3. Joey's end of the see-saw goes _______. Coco's ______ goes ______. Coco shoots ______ into the air.

4. Coco takes hold of a ________.

Word-bank

climbs
down
end
jumps
see-saw
stands
steps
swing
up

What happens next?

• **Draw the next picture. Write a sentence.**

Teachers' note Ask the children to describe orally what the clowns do. Encourage them to use accurate vocabulary, such as 'lands', 'see-saw', 'jumps' and 'swing' (or 'trapeze'). Point out the causes and effects of what happens: for example, Coco's end of the see-saw goes up because Joey lands on the other end.

A tomato plant

- **Look at the** life-cycle **of a tomato.**
- **Read the sentences about each part of the** diagram**. Fill in the gaps.**

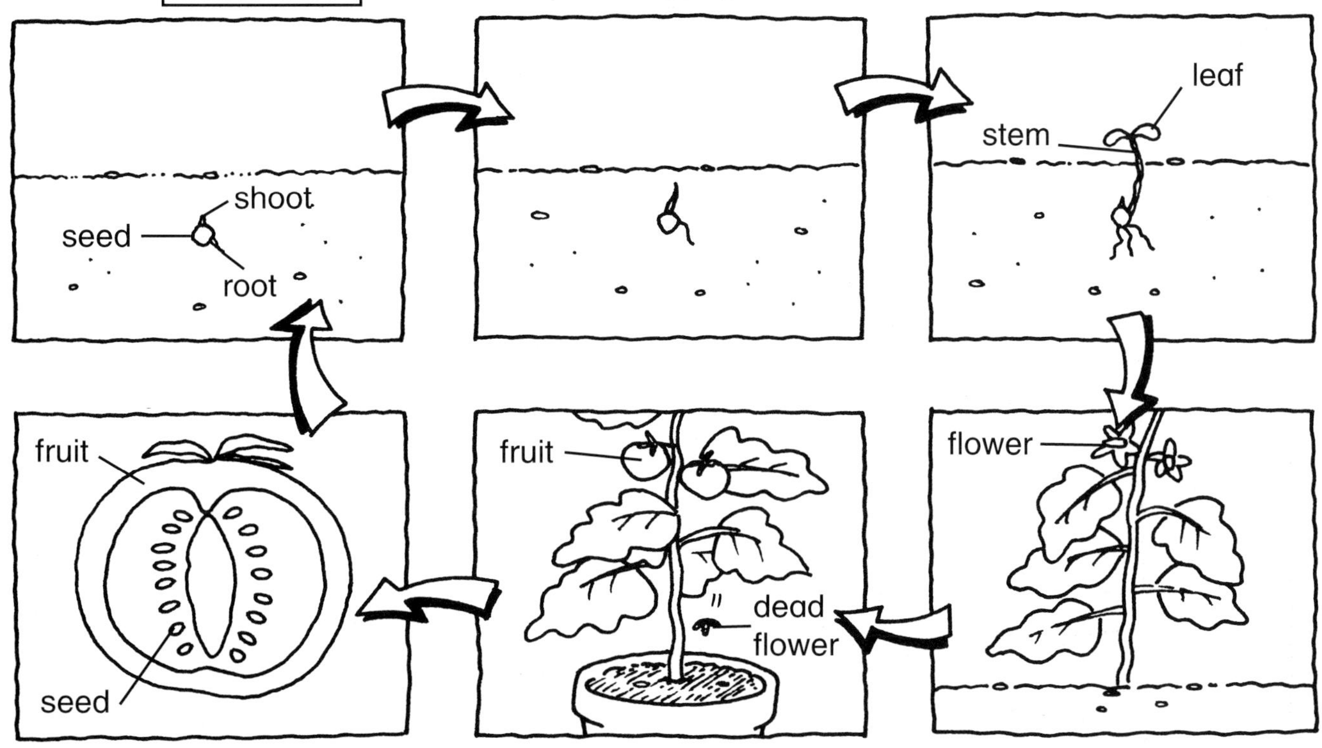

a. A root grows downwards from the __________.

b. A shoot ____________ upwards from the ____________.

c. Leaves grow __________________________________.

d. The stem grows __________ and flowers ____.

e. The flowers die and ________________. Fruit ____.

f. Inside the fruit ____.

Teachers' note At the start of the activity, help the children to explain orally what happens as the tomato plant grows. Ensure the children understand the continuous nature of the cycle. Encourage them to use the vocabulary provided on this page and to say in which direction the root and the shoot grow. You could write the words 'upwards' and 'downwards' on the board.

Fact or fiction?

Facts are true. Fiction is made up.

- **Write whether each sentence is fact or fiction.**

The troll was hiding under the bridge.

fiction

An acorn is the fruit of an oak tree.

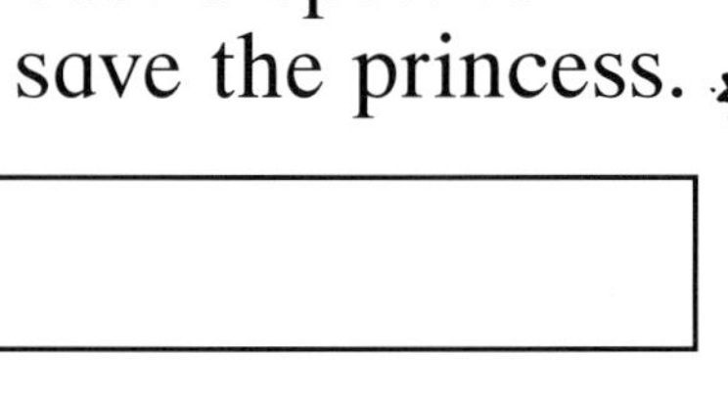

The good fairy cast a spell to save the princess.

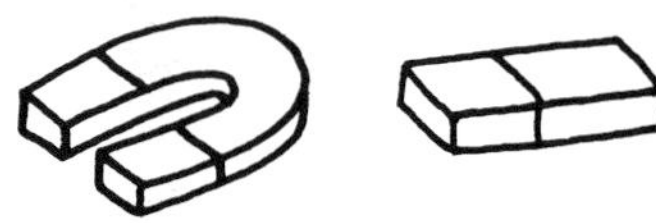

Magnets can have different shapes.

In the mud was a single huge footprint with three claws.

The little bear climbed up a moonbeam.

Snowflakes have six points. No two snowflakes are the same.

- **Write two more sentences which are facts.**
- **Write two more sentences which are fiction.**

Teachers' note Explain the terms 'fact' and 'fiction', and show the children examples of each. You could read out sentences from fiction and non-fiction books and play a game similar to 'Simon says'. The children put up their hands after a sentence which is 'fact' but not after one which is 'fiction'.

Fiction or non-fiction?

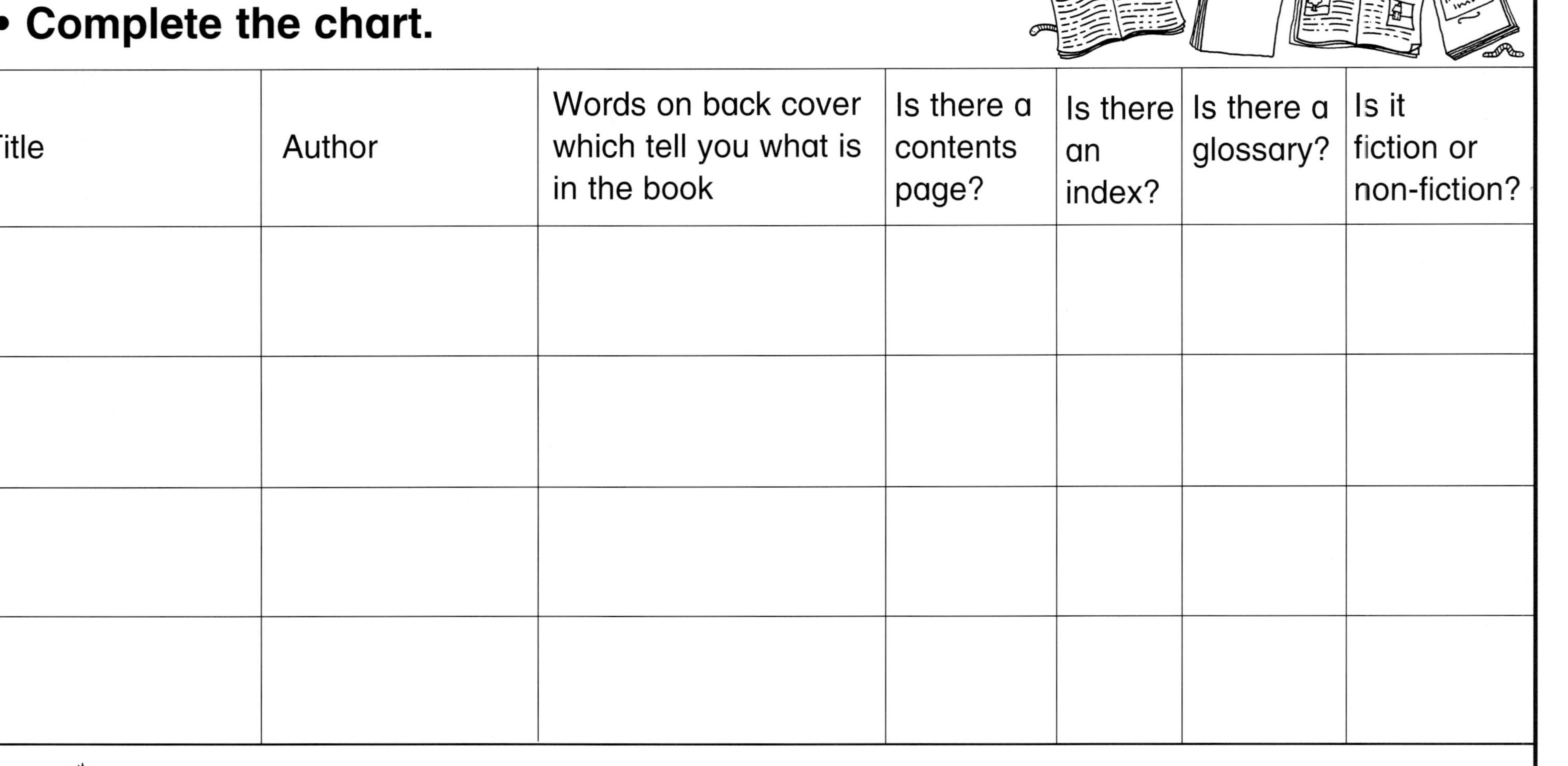

- Look at four different books in your classroom.
- Complete the chart.

Title	Author	Words on back cover which tell you what is in the book	Is there a contents page?	Is there an index?	Is there a glossary?	Is it fiction or non-fiction?

Now try this!

- Write the titles of three other non-fiction books.
- Write what each book is about.

Teachers' note You could begin by holding up a book; ask the children to look at the front and back covers and to decide whether it is fiction or non-fiction. Draw attention to the important features of non-fiction books. For this activity, the children should work in small groups. Each group needs a selection of fiction and non-fiction books.

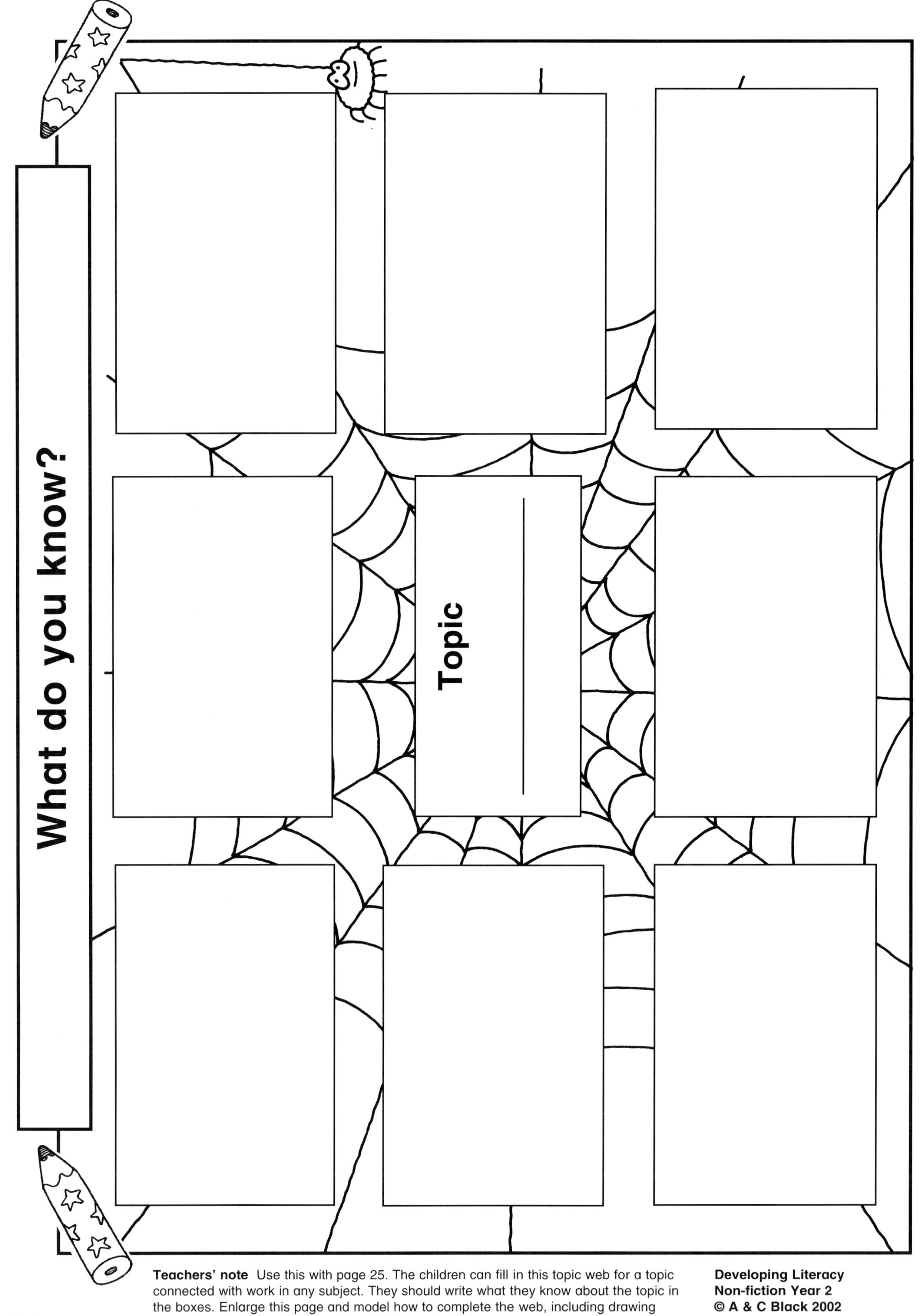

Teachers' note Use this with page 25. The children can fill in this topic web for a topic connected with work in any subject. They should write what they know about the topic in the boxes. Enlarge this page and model how to complete the web, including drawing arrows to join pieces of information which are related to one another.

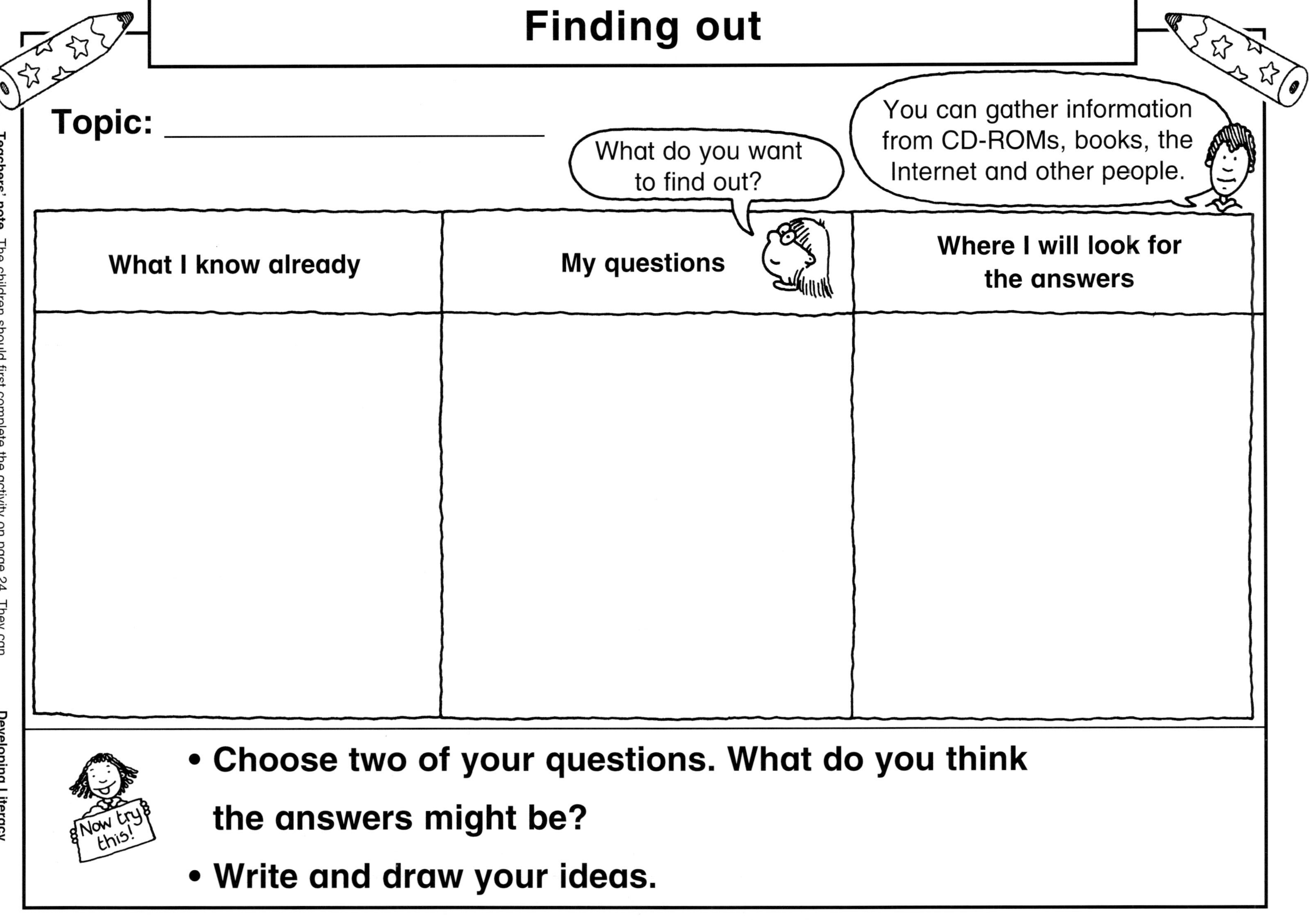

Teachers' note The children should first complete the activity on page 24. They can transfer some of their statements from page 24 into the first column ('What I know already') and then write questions to enable them to find out more, or to check if their knowledge of the topic is correct. Discuss the other sources the children could use besides books.

What's the answer?

- **Read the children's questions.**

How did people make their castles strong?

What plants grow in Antarctica?

How do Hindus celebrate Divali?

- **Choose books which might help the children.**
- **Check the contents page, sub-headings, illustrations and index.**
- **Fill in the chart.**

Question	**Title of book**	**Will the book help? List useful pages.**
How did people make their castles strong?		
What plants grow in Antarctica?		
How do Hindus celebrate Divali?		

- **Think of a question of your own.**
- **Draw a chart like the one on this page.**
- **Fill in your chart.**

Teachers' note The children should first complete the activities on pages 24 and 25. You could begin by modelling how to find the answer to another question (for instance, 'What makes it rain?'). Show a selection of books and ask the children which ones might help and how they can tell. Model how to check books to see if they will be useful.

Find the information

Topic ____________________

My question ____________________

____

Book title ____________________

____

Look at the contents page.

Useful chapters		
Chapter number	Chapter heading	Page

Useful sub-headings	
Sub-heading	Page

Useful index words	
Word	Pages

- **Write the answer to your question.**

Teachers' note The children should first have completed the activities on pages 24–26. Choose one of the books used to introduce the previous activity and model how to skim it quickly to find the information needed. A useful way of doing this is to carry out the process while 'thinking aloud' about what you are doing.

Text scan

- **Read Mair and Jay's chart.**

Topic Birds		
What we already know	**What we want to know**	**Where we will look to find out**
Some birds go away in the winter.	Why do the birds go away? Where do they go?	'See for yourself: Snow and Ice' by Kay Davies and Wendy Oldfield

The children think page 18 will help them.

- **Read the text.**
- **Underline the important words.**

Animals in winter

It is hard for birds to find food in winter. The blackbird in the picture is looking for food in the snow. Many of the insects and plants that birds eat die in cold weather. If ponds freeze, it is hard for birds to find water to drink.

A blackbird

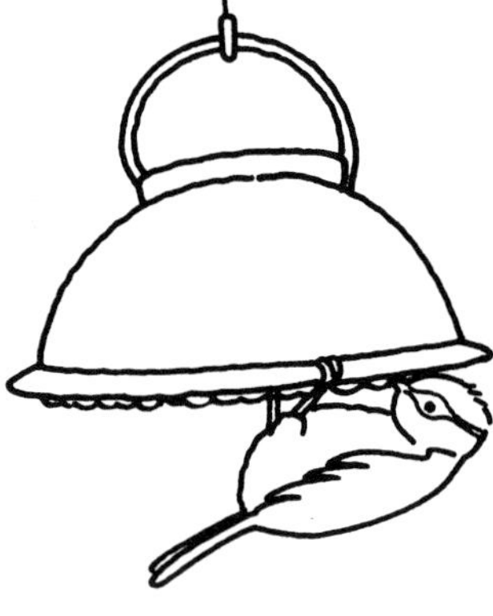

Some birds fly away to warmer countries for the winter, where there are plenty of insects to eat.

You can give birds water and food. Mix nuts and seeds with fat. Put the mixture into something like this bell or half a coconut shell. Let the mixture set. Hang it up outside with a piece of string.

18

- **Find another useful book for the children.**
- **Look for a helpful page.**
- **Write the important words from the page.**

Teachers' note The children should first have completed the activities on pages 24–27. Introduce the activity by reading the chart with the children. Ask them what topic the children in the activity are working on, what they know about it, what they want to find out and where they are going to look. Encourage the children to consider how Mair and Jay knew that page 18 in the book would help them.

A journey

- **Look at the map and the key. They show how Greg goes to visit his cousin Lisa.**

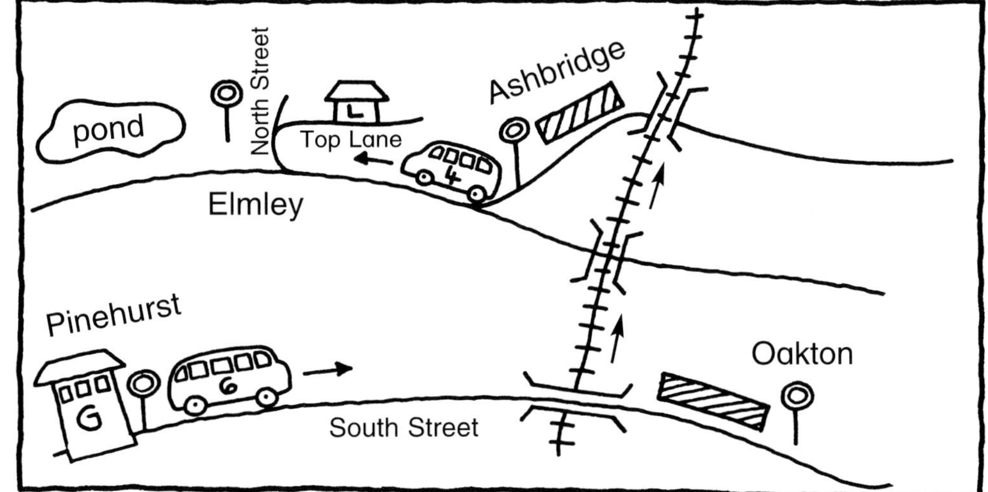

- **Write instructions for Greg.**

1. From your house, walk along South Street to the ________ ________.

2. Take the number ___ bus to ____________.

3. Get off the ________ at the railway ____________.

4. Take the ________ to ______________.

5. Take the number ___ ________ from Ashbridge railway station to ____________.

6. Get off the bus at ____________ Street.

7. Cross the road and turn right into ______________.

- **Write instructions for Lisa to go to Greg's house.**

You might need to turn the map upside-down.

Teachers' note It will be helpful to revise the use of keys, and to invite the children to describe what they can see on the map. For lower-achieving children, you could add words to the skeleton instructions; for higher-achieving children, you may wish to delete some of those provided.

Grotty soup

Mr Grott is making a cauldron of grotty soup.

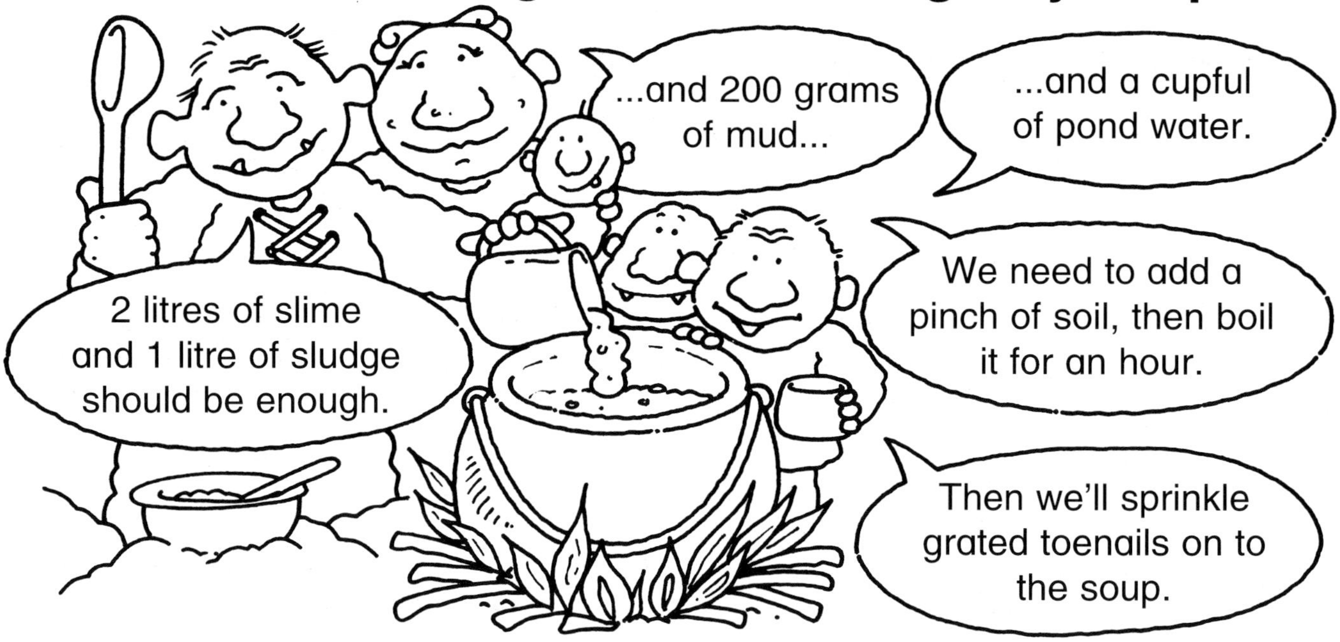

...and 200 grams of mud...

...and a cupful of pond water.

2 litres of slime and 1 litre of sludge should be enough.

We need to add a pinch of soil, then boil it for an hour.

Then we'll sprinkle grated toenails on to the soup.

- **Write the recipe for Mr Grott's soup.**

Ingredients:

2 litres slime

Method: Put the slime and

- **Write a recipe for grotty sandwiches.**

Teachers' note The children should first read some recipes and notice their key features: a list of ingredients and, sometimes, equipment, followed by step-by-step instructions which use direct language to tell the reader what to do. You could introduce the activity by inviting a group of children to read the parts of 'the Grotts' and the narrator.

Snakes and ladders

- **Look at the pictures.**
- **Read the labels and captions.**

- **Complete the instructions.**

1. Roll the dice________.

2. Look at the ________. Move that number of squares.

3. If you ________________________________,

go ________________________________.

4. If you ________________________________,

go ________________________________.

5. Give the __________ and the __________ to

the ________________________.

6. The winner ________________________________.

- **Draw pictures for another game.**
- **Write instructions.**

Teachers' note This could be introduced by reading the instructions for another familiar game as a shared text. Discuss the important features of instructions for games: telling the readers, step-by-step, what to do, what they should do if different things happen in the game, how their turn ends and how to win.

Sending a letter

- **Write instructions for sending a letter.**

Word-bank

address	name	stamp
envelope	post	stick
letter	postbox	to

1. Fold the letter.
2. Put the letter ______________________.
3. Write ______________________

______________________.
4. ______________________.
5. ______________________.

- **Write instructions for sending a birthday present.**

____

____

____

____

____

____

Word-bank

address
from
label
name
paper
post office
stick
sticky tape
take
to
wrap
write

Teachers' note It may be useful for the children first to act out the process of sending a letter, while telling a friend what they are doing. Before the extension activity they could act out the wrapping and sending of a present. As a further extension activity, ask the children to write instructions for sending e-mails to pen-friends in other schools.

Follow a diagram

- **Label the diagram.**
- **Complete the instructions for making the** circuit.

Word-bank

battery	battery-holder
bulb	bulb-holder
electricity	join
off	on
switch	wire

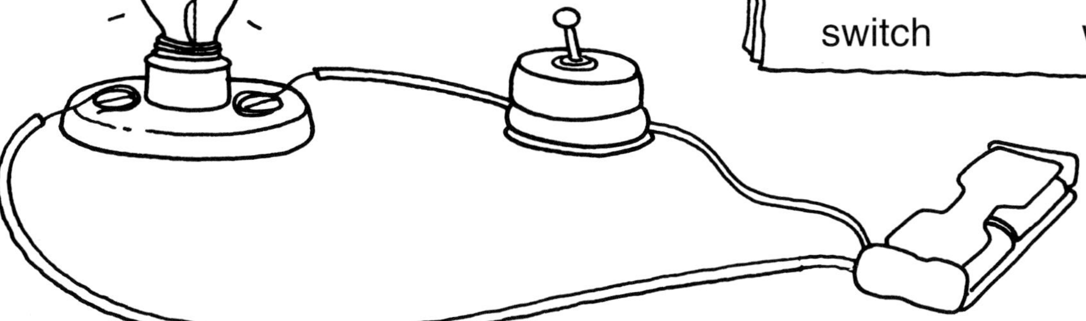

You need: a bulb, ____________________

____

____

1. Join one wire from the battery-holder to the ________.
2. Join the other wire to the ________________.
3. Join a wire from the switch to the ________________.
4. Screw a bulb into the ________________.
5. Switch on ________________.

- **Write three questions about the diagram.**
- **Give them to a friend to answer.**

For example:
How many bulbs do I need?

Teachers' note The children first need experience of using a simple circuit with a switch. Discuss the words in the word-bank; you may wish to show the children the relevant equipment as a reminder. Invite them to explain what happens when they switch on and off. Their explanations need not involve scientific knowledge at great depth, but could be based simply on their observations.

Instruction words

- **Read how Emma made a magnetic fishing set.**

1.

I drew 10 fish.

2.

I cut out the fish.

3.

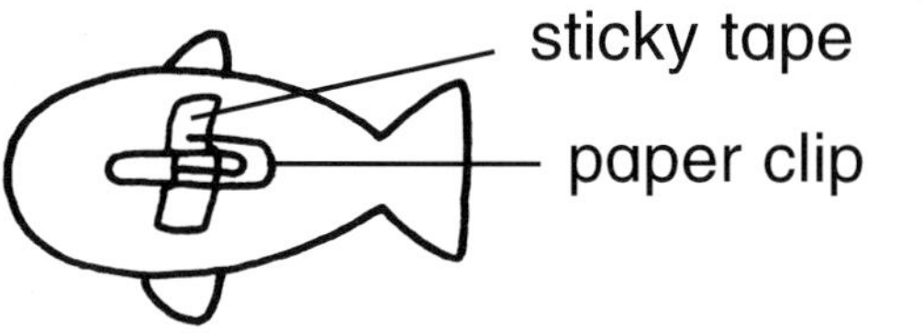

I taped a paper clip on to each fish.

4.

I tied a piece of string on to a magnet.

Turn Emma's writing into instructions.

- **Underline the words you need to change.**
- **Write the instructions.**

Do not use the word 'I'.

How to make a magnetic fishing set

You need: a pencil, ____________________

____

1. Draw ____________________

2. ____________________

3. ____________________

4. ____________________

- **Write instructions for playing the game.**

Teachers' note Read to the class the recount about making a magnetic fishing set. Ask the children if it sounds like a set of instructions (whether it tells the reader what to do). Model how to change the first sentence to direct language. For the extension activity, remind the children to start each sentence with an instruction word.

Joke dictionary 1

- **Match the words to the joke definitions.**
- **Write the words in the joke dictionary.**

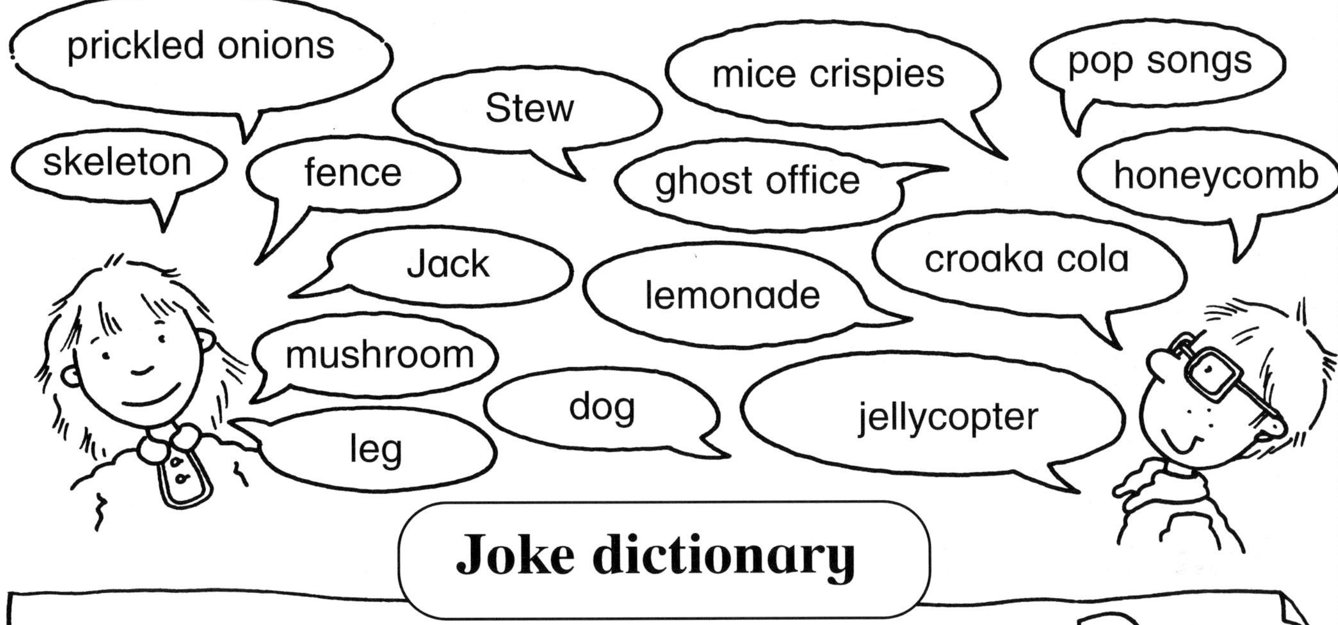

Joke dictionary

bulldozer ______ A sleeping bull. 

______ A drink for frogs. 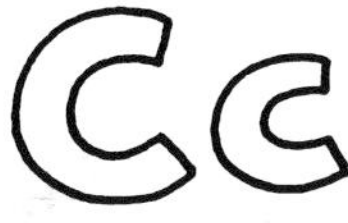

______ An animal which has a coat and pants. 

______ Something which can go round a field without moving. 

______ A place where spooks buy stamps. 

Teachers' note Use this with page 36. You could introduce the activity by asking the children to give the answers to jokes: for example, 'What do you get when you cross a sheep and a kangaroo?' – 'A woolly jumper'. Model how to make definitions from the jokes (ask them for the definition of a woolly jumper: a cross between a sheep and a kangaroo). Continued on page 36.

Joke dictionary 2

________________	A hairdressing tool for bees.
________________	A man with a car on his head.
________________	A wobbly flying machine.
________________	Something which has a bottom at the top.
________________	First aid for lemons.
________________	A cat's breakfast.
________________	The world's smallest room.
________________	Dad's tunes.
________________	A hedgehog's favourite food.
________________	Someone who has nobody to talk to.
________________	A man with a saucepan on his head.

- **Write three more joke definitions.**

Teachers' note Continued from page 35. Before the lesson, the children could be asked to bring in books of jokes and examples of 'definition' jokes. They could make a class dictionary of joke definitions in a word-processed table, and then use the sorting function on the computer to arrange the definitions in alphabetical order. Encourage them to notice what happens to words beginning with the same letter.

Famous names

- **Fill in the gaps in the directory.**

Use information books.

Florence Nightingale | Guy Fawkes | Mary Seacole | Samuel Pepys

F

Name	Famous events	Dates
Guy Fawkes		

N

Name	Famous events	Dates

P

Name	Famous events	Dates

S

Name	Famous events	Dates

Now try this!

- **Make directory cards for other people in history.**

The Tudors

Teachers' note Introduce the activity by asking the children what they know about each of the people depicted. Make a note of their responses and ask them what they need to find out about each person in order to complete the directory. Encourage them to suggest what sources they can use to find the information.

Fairground glossary

- **Think of different kinds of fairground rides.**
- **Write the name of each ride on a glossary card.**

- **Write a definition. Draw a picture.**
- **Put the cards in alphabetical order.**

roller coaster

A car running up and down slopes on a track.

dodgems

Cars which run by electricity. You drive them in a special area.

A giant's flow-chart

- **Design a 'people trap' for the giant.**
- **Draw pictures. Write labels and notes.**

What should the giant do next?

- **Draw and write the next part of the flow-chart.**

Teachers' note Discuss what the children know about giants in stories. Ask them how a giant could set a trap to catch people and draw their attention to the questions on this page, which will help them to organise their flow-chart.

Gran's schooldays 1

The children asked Laura's gran about her schooldays in the 1940s.

- **Read their questions and notes.**

Questions	Notes
 Did you have felt-tipped pens?	No felt-tips. No ballpoint pens. Pen – wooden handle, metal nib. Dipped in ink. Ink in pot in hole in desktop. Pencil crayons.
 What subjects did you learn?	Eng. Maths. Nature study. Art. PT (phys. training). Girls – needlework. Boys – handicraft.
 What was your uniform like?	Navy blue gymslip, cardigan, white blouse, school tie, white ankle-socks. Black or brown lace-up shoes. Navy blue blazer + beret.
 What did the boys wear?	Grey shorts, pullover, white shirt, school tie, grey knee-socks. Black or brown lace-up shoes. Navy blue blazer + cap.
 What did you do at lunchtime?	School dinner 6d. each (old money) – or go home. No packed lunch. 12.00–1.30.

Teachers' note Use this with page 41. The children might need to use dictionaries and information books to find the meanings of some of the words in the notes. It may be necessary to revise how to use glossaries and indexes for this.

Gran's schooldays 2

- **Write about Laura's gran's schooldays.**

School in the 1940s

Writing

In the 1940s ______________________________

____

____

Subjects

Girls and boys both learned ______________________________

____

____

Girls' uniform

Laura's gran wore ______________________________

____

____

Boys' uniform

Boys wore ______________________________

____

____

Lunch

At lunchtime children ______________________________

____

____

Teachers' note Use this with page 40. Draw attention to how the sub-headings have come from the questions on page 40. The children could underline the key words in the questions. In their other work, in history and other subjects, they could look for key words in the questions they pose, and use these words for sub-headings.

Making notes 1

- **Write the information in the shortest way you can.**

You can miss out words like me, I, we and my.

I went to the park on Sunday.

Sun – went → park

Shortened words

afternoon	pm
and	+
evening	pm
football	f'ball
morning	am
seven	7
Sunday	Sun
to	→

In the morning I played football with my Mum.

After that we had fish and chips for lunch.

In the afternoon we went to visit my Gran.

We got home at seven o'clock in the evening.

- **Make notes about something you have done.**

Teachers' note Discuss the purpose of making notes and point out that notes are meant to be written quickly, for personal use, to be written up later for others to read. You could show the children examples of good and bad note-making: good notes can be read and understood later; bad notes cannot. Point out that in notes it is quicker not to write full sentences.

Making notes 2

- **Read Sunhil's question.**
- **Read the text.**
- **Underline the parts which will help Sunhil to answer the question.**

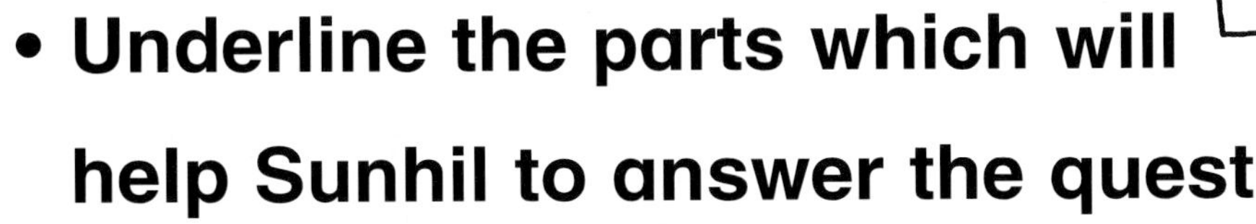

Fish are cold-blooded. This means that the body of a fish has the same temperature as the water around it. A fish's body is covered with scales.

All animals need a gas called oxygen. There is oxygen in the air and in water. People, and many other animals, use their lungs to breathe in oxygen from the air. In their lungs oxygen passes into the blood.

The heart pumps the blood, with the oxygen in it, around the body.

A fish does not have lungs. It cannot breathe in oxygen from the air. Instead, it has gills behind its head. Water goes into the fish's mouth, over the gills and back out through the gills. In the gills, oxygen is taken from the water into the blood.

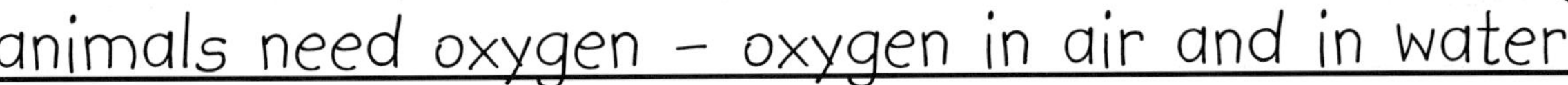

- **Make notes about how fish breathe.**

animals need oxygen – oxygen in air and in water

- **Cover the text.**

- **Write an explanation of how fish breathe.**

Teachers' note The children should first complete the activity on page 42. Explain that this activity is about finding the information needed to answer a question, and about making notes only on the words and phrases which will help them. Remind the children that notes need to be written in the shortest and quickest way possible. They could compare their notes with the sentences in the report.

Topic word lists

- **Read the words.**
- **Look at the pictures.**
- **Write the words on the correct lists.**

Space	Toys	Monsters
a stronaut	ball	alien
c ______	car	gh ______
Earth	d ______	gi ______
meteor	kaleidoscope	King Kong
M ______	p ______	t ______
planet	r ______	unicorn
r ______	snakes and ladders	v ______
satellite	te ______	witch
s ______	t ______	y ______

Teachers' note You could begin by discussing words connected with a topic the children have been learning about. Point out that topic word lists help them to remember new words. They can also be used for looking up spellings.

Silly lists

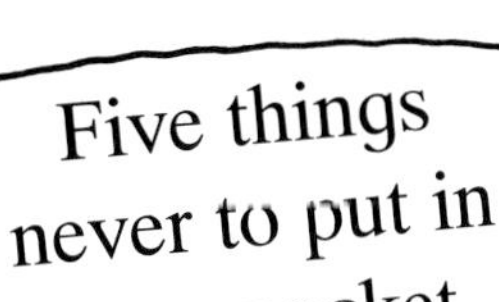

An eel, an ice cream, an elephant, a football and a jelly.

Use commas, except before **and**.

- **Write your own silly lists.**

Five things a snail cannot learn to do

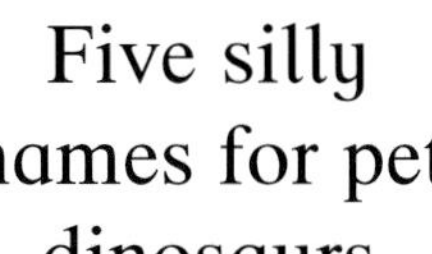

Five silly names for pet dinosaurs

Five things not to wear when swimming

Five things found in a witch's handbag

- **Re-write your lists in alphabetical order.**

Teachers' note You could revise commas with the class by writing a list without any commas in it and then reading it aloud. Ask the children what was wrong with the list and what would help you to read it properly. Point out that a comma is not needed before the last item in a list and ask them which word is used instead ('and').

Write a report

- **Help Daniel to improve his report.**

I saw some trees in the park. I saw some ducks on the pond. I saw an oak tree. I saw a frog by the pond. I saw swings in the playground in the park. I saw a dragonfly by the pond. I saw a see-saw in the playground. I saw a willow tree and a beech tree in the park. I saw climbing frames in the playground.

- **Use the plan to help you re-write the report.**

What is the report about?

Heading ____________________

Sub-heading ____________________

I saw ____________________.

There was an ______________, a ______________

and a ____________________.

Sub-heading ____________________

I saw some animals by the __________.

There was a ______________,

a ______________ and some __________.

Sub-heading ____________________

In the playground I saw ____________________,

a ______________ and ____________________.

- **Think of useful words for starting sentences in a report. Make a list.**

Examples: There is | There are | I saw

Teachers' note Read the report with the children. Ask them what it is about and what heading they could give it. Point out that it is rather mixed up, because the writer has not grouped the different kinds of things he saw. Ask the children to look for groups of things, such as trees.

Using a chart

- **List as many different types of building as you can.**

Use information books.

barn, theatre, flats, factory,

- **Write the names of the buildings on the chart.**

Buildings			
Homes	**Leisure**	**Storage**	**Business**
flats	theatre	barn	factory

- **Make a chart for listing different kinds of furniture. Fill it in.**

Teachers' note When the children have completed the chart, encourage them to think of ways it could help them to plan a report about buildings. Ask them to suggest what sub-headings they could use in the report.

An experiment

- **Look at the pictures.**
- **Write about what the children did.**

1.

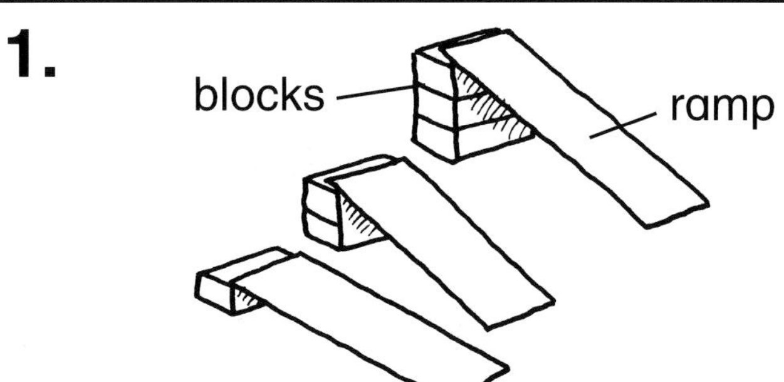

2.

3.

4.

First, the children ____________________

____

____

____

____

____

____

____

Word-bank

first
to begin
next
after that
then
finally
lastly

- **Write about an experiment you have done.**

Teachers' note Introduce the activity by discussing the purpose of the experiment (to find out how the height of a ramp affects the distance travelled by a toy car). Discuss the difference between describing what was done during an experiment and writing up the results. The children could plan a table for recording the results of an experiment.